Birds of
Paradise

Written by Don Harper
Illustrated by David Thelwell

TOP THAT! Kids™

Published by Top That! Publishing Inc.
25031 W. Avenue Stanford, Suite # 60, Valencia, CA 91355
www.topthatpublishing.com
Copyright © 2005 Top That! Publishing plc
Top That! Kids is a trademark of Top That! Publishing plc

0 2 4 6 8 9 7 5 3 1
Printed and bound in China

Life in the Rainforest

Tropical rainforests are home to some of the strangest and most beautiful birds in the world. All areas of rainforest lie on, or near, the broadest part of Earth, the center, known as the equator.

Dense Foliage

Rainforests can be dark and gloomy places due to the dense layer of tall trees forming what is known as the canopy.

Top facts...

The largest area of rainforest in the world is the Amazon, in South America, but there are other rainforests in Africa, Asia, and Australia.

The annual rainfall can exceed 8 feet in tropical rainforest areas.

Nearly half the world's tropical rainforest has been destroyed during the last 40 years.

Water drips down through the leaves on to the forest floor where mosses and other moisture-loving plants grow. It feels hot and steamy.

Living up High

Some birds, such as giant hornbills, live in the upper part of the rainforest, feeding on fruits and flowers in the tall trees. Birds are important to rainforest plants because, by eating their fruit, they carry seeds in their bodies which are then passed out in droppings to grow as new plants elsewhere in the forest.

Eggs

With many birds of paradise, the hen is responsible not just for building the nest, but also hatching and looking after the chicks on her own. She usually only lays one or two eggs which are attractively marked, often with reddish, mauve, or brown patterning.

Hatching Chicks

Some birds of paradise do form pairs and, in these cases, the male stays with the female as she builds the nest and helps to provide food once the chicks have hatched.

Top facts...

In northern Australia, trumpet manucodes often choose a nest site near those of black butcherbirds. This is because the fierce nature of the butcherbirds serves to keep away would-be predators, and so helps to ensure the safety of manucodes nesting nearby.

The king bird of paradise is unusual in that it nests in a hole in a hollow tree.

Spectacularly Beautiful Birds

Their ornate plumage and dazzling courtship displays means birds of paradise are sometimes called "birds of the gods."

Greater Bird of Paradise

During the late 1800s, up to 30,000 birds of paradise, such as the greater bird of paradise, were killed each year for their feathers. These were sent to Europe and used to decorate hats. By the time this trade was outlawed in the 1920s, it is thought some birds of paradise had become extinct.

One wealthy man, called Sir. Richard Ingram, was so worried about the survival of the greater bird of paradise that, in 1908, he arranged for about 50 of these birds to be moved to the other side of the world to a tropical island which he had purchased, called Little Tobago. Remarkably, they survived here and bred for about 70 years, but they are thought to have died out in the early 1980s after a hurricane blew down much of the forest on this Caribbean island.

Did you know?
Birds of paradise first became known in Europe during the 1500s simply as skins, with their legs and feet removed. It was believed they had no legs and so never perched. This gave rise to the story that the hen laid her eggs which were carried by the cock bird on his back.

Red Bird of Paradise

When they fly, the wings of these birds of paradise create a rustling sound. As part of their display, cock birds flap their wings, drawing the hen's attention to the crimson area of feathering. They display high up in the trees in groups of as many as ten males. One of the features of male red birds of paradise is the presence of shiny green feathers on their heads. Some of these can be raised during their display, to create the impression of horns on their head. These displays are most commonly seen during the early part of the morning.

Did you know?

Native tribespeople traditionally hunted birds of paradise for their fantastic plumes, making these into headdresses and other garments.

Paradise Riflebird

Paradise riflebirds are one of the Australian birds of paradise. Their long, and slightly curved, bills allow them to seek out insects and spiders which hide in small tree holes and under bark. They are very agile birds with strong feet which enable them to hop straight up a tree without losing their grip. It takes at least four years for young cock birds to obtain adult plumage but, unusually, they may actually breed while they are still

in immature feathering. Groups of males display from open sites, called stages, up in the forest canopy. Young paradise riflebirds have black skin and no covering of warm, downy feathers when they hatch.

Black Sicklebill

When displaying, the cock bird fans out the tufts of feathers on the sides of his chest, which makes him look rather like he has arms. He also spreads out his tail feathers slightly to show how these vary in length, with the top one being the longest. Males also undertake display flights, diving down towards the ground and swooping back up to a branch again.

Young male black sicklebills look like adult hens when they first leave the nest, and they moult in a very specific way. They start to obtain the dark head coloration of adult cocks at first, with this color change spreading down over the body over successive molts. The last parts of the body to be transformed are the wings and the area between the legs.

Did you know?

Black sicklebills are the largest birds of paradise, measuring 43 inches with a tail of 30 inches.

King of Saxony Bird of Paradise

Although the cock birds are more colorful than the hens, it's their long plumes that make them unique. These have been likened to the fronds of ferns, extending back from behind their eyes. Even more remarkably, they can be extended in virtually any direction, so that one of these magnificent plumes may point upwards, while the other points downwards.

Their display begins with the cock bird starting to bounce on a perch. The hen then joins in so that they jump up into the air together for a few seconds at a time. They then pause and look at each other before repeating these movements several times in succession. The cock bird then holds his plumes forwards over his head before mating occurs.

Top facts...

In the late 1800s it was considered a great honor to have your name associated with a bird of paradise and, in this case, the bird is named after the King of Saxony.

Other Exotic Rainforest Species

Many of the birds living in the world's rainforests are found nowhere else—they have no need to migrate from one country to another because they live in an environment where food is readily available throughout the year.

Philippine Eagle

The largest predatory birds fly over the canopy, and will seize not only other birds but also animals, such as monkeys. The gigantic Philippine eagle actually used to be called the monkey-eating eagle for this reason. It has now become very scarce, largely because of the clearance of rainforest on the Philippine islands where it lives.

Pigeons and Doves

Colorful fruit-eating pigeons and doves are to be found alongside birds of paradise in the rainforests of New Guinea and Australia, as well as on other islands in this region of the world. Pied imperial-pigeons migrate from New Guinea to northern Australia each summer to breed, and rely on a steady supply of fruit from rainforest trees to sustain them.

Did you know?

The difficulties of exploring the rainforest mean that birds which were previously unknown are still being discovered in these areas around the world. During the 1980s alone, three new parrots were discovered in the Amazon region, with another being reported for the first time in 2002.

Blue Crowned Pigeon

Many birds which live on the floor of the rainforest often prefer to walk, only flying as a last resort if they are frightened. They include the beautiful blue crowned pigeons which are only found in the rainforests of New Guinea. Growing to the size of large chickens, these birds have attractive lace-like crests on their heads.

Three-wattled Bellbird

The calls of the three-wattled bellbird of the Amazon rainforest are especially loud, and sound like the ringing of a bell. They can be heard over the background noise in the rainforest from a distance of more than a mile.

Double-wattled Cassowary

These birds are the giants of the forest and are fearsome if cornered. Cassowaries feed largely on fruits and berries, as well as insects. They live in the rainforests of New Guinea and neighboring islands, as well as in northern Australia. The distinctive swollen area on the head of a cassowary is known as the casque. It is thought that this acts rather like a helmet, allowing them to run through the forest with their head down, yet avoiding any risk of serious injury. These cassowaries also have a pair of fleshy swellings, known as wattles, on the neck which are formed by folds of skin.

Top fact...
Double-wattled cassowaries are known to stand over 6 feet tall. If cornered, they will strike out with their powerful feet, which consist of three toes. The shorter, inner toe is equipped with a sharp claw which acts like a sword. This is capable of ripping a man's body open with a single blow, and injuries of this type have killed people.

Hoatzins

Found in the Amazon region of South America, hoatzins have features which they share with some of the earliest birds. These are most evident in their young, which are very alert from an early age and will jump down out of their nests if danger threatens.

Hoatzins feed largely on vegetation, rather than fruit or seeds. Since leaves provide them with little energy, they are forced to eat large amounts. Hoatzins have a very large organ, known as a crop, at the base of their neck. Leaves are stored in the crop after they are swallowed but before they enter the hoatzin's stomach where they are finally broken down. After eating, a hoatzin's crop may bulge so much that it has difficulty in flying. They are not strong fliers in any case, preferring to glide from tree to tree as necessary.

Did you know?
These primitive birds have a musky odor which makes them smell very unpleasant.

Toco Toucan

Toucans generally have long, broad and colorful bills, with that of the toco being the largest and brightest of all.

Toco toucans live in South America, feeding in the treetops on fruit, as well as eggs and chicks stolen from the nests of other birds. They rely on their long beak to obtain food which would otherwise be out of reach. The rough edges, known as serrations, running along the edges of the toucan's bill, help these birds to grip their food. If the food is too large to swallow, they will hold it against a perch and pull off pieces. These pieces are then tossed into the air before being caught and swallowed.

Top facts...
A toco toucan's bill is approximately 8 inches long— equivalent to a third of its total body length.

at Hornbill

reat hornbill is the largest member of the hornbill group measuring 4 feet in length, and is found in western India and parts of south-east Asia.

Pairs breed in tree holes, with both the cock and hen working together to seal the entrance hole using droppings, bark and other material. Just a slit is left through which the male feeds his partner as she incubates the eggs.

He may regurgitate up to 50 grape-sized fruits on each visit to the nest and also brings animal food, especially once the chicks have hatched. The female stays walled-up in the nest until the young hornbills are well grown. She then breaks out, and the chicks seal the nest again behind her. It is thought this behavior has developed to keep out snakes which could prey on the young birds.

Top facts...
Hornbills are unusual amongst birds in having what appear to be long eyelashes, although these are actually modified feathers which may help to keep dust out of their eyes.